Protection

Michelle Lerner

A Publication of The Poetry Box®

Editing & Book Design by Shawn Aveningo Sanders
Cover Design by Shawn Aveningo Sanders
Cover Photograph by Robert R. Sanders
(RobertSandersPhoto.com)

ISBN: 978-1-948461-88-7
Printed in the United States of America.
Wholesale distribution via Ingram Group.

Published by The Poetry Box®, 2021
Portland, Oregon
ThePoetryBox.com

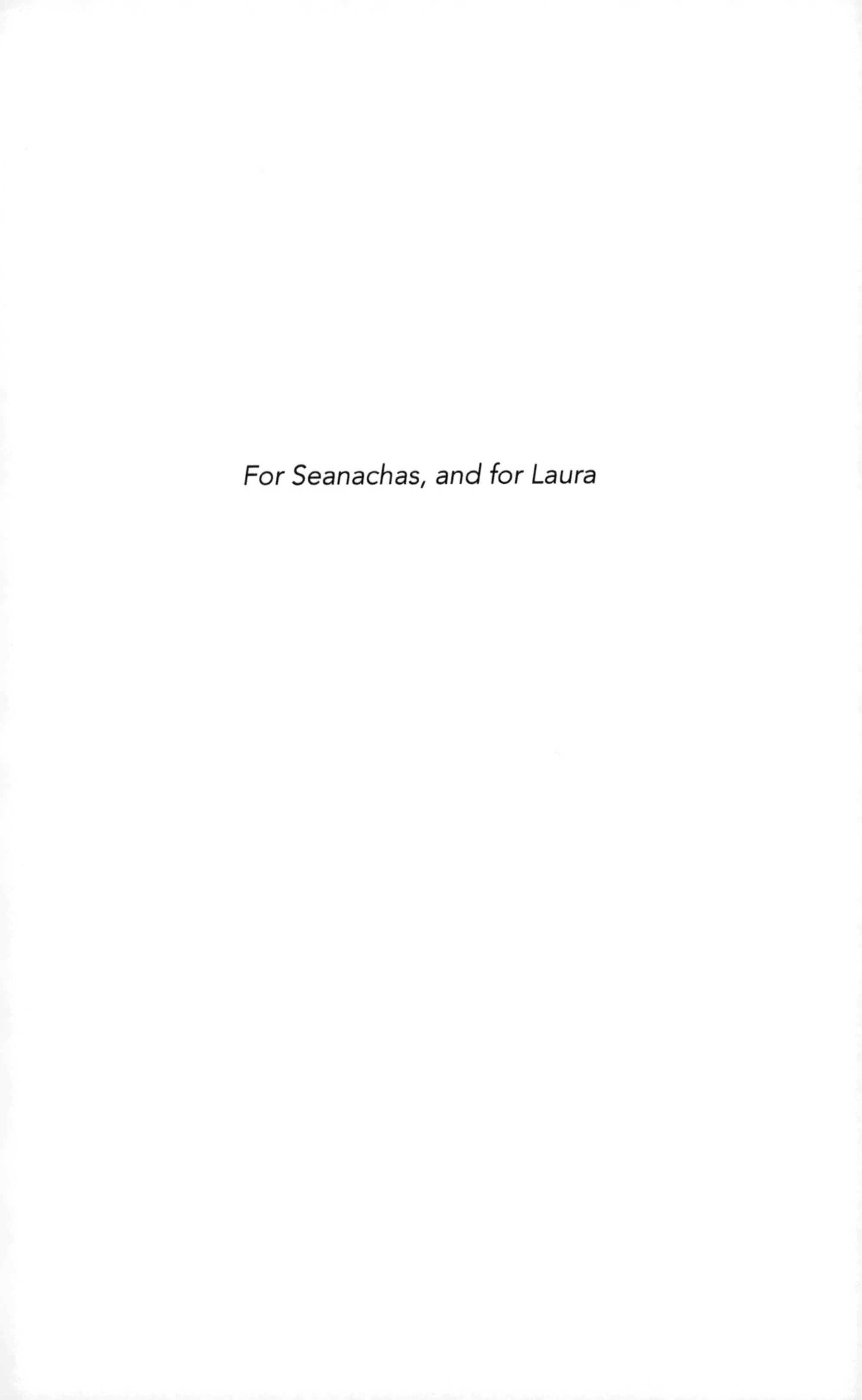

For Seanachas, and for Laura

A Note about Pronouns

The poems in this book track my experiences parenting a gender expansive child from infancy to age 6. My child in later years realized that they are nonbinary and chose to use the pronouns they/them. Out of respect, I considered going back and changing the pronouns in the poems to match their current gender identity and preferences. However, I found that doing so made some of the poems seem inauthentic and confusing, as they are in part about the ambiguity and conflict surrounding the pronouns we used at the time. In the end, with my child's blessing, I decided to leave the pronouns as they were originally written, with a nod to the fact that our experience of gender is fluid and can develop and change over time.

Contents

House

I am your tin house,
your cabin, your tent
and like a tiny nomad you travel with your yurt
on your back, wrapping around you
as you writhe like a bronco, bucking at the walls
my blood just the whisper
of wind as you stretch.

You do not know yet to be lonely
you do not know
what it means
to wait.

I am a house of spirits,
yours and mine.
You hiccup and I try
to hold you in, to hold you still
with my hand on the roof of your world.

And your father surrounds me
as I surround you,
he is my house
opens windows and doors
offers me his arms, offers me his back.
Sometimes he holds you at night,
his hand on my belly, cupped
around your foot, or fist
as you sleep unknowing,
his hands not really hands,

[. . .]

his voice just vibrations
of the air in the eaves
of your tin house, your tent,
this space that I have given you
this room of your own
to stretch into the world
creating
yourself
as we watch, wide-eyed, and wait.

I'll Tell You How It Was

I'll tell you how it was:
the water flooded
between my knees
poured out and out, over the metal bed
onto the floor.
I removed everything
the bed sheets the gown
myself from the bed
the mask of complacency
every thread
of inhibition.
"She likes to be naked" the nurses said
as you bore down in me
harder, farther
than they warned
scooping out my insides, making room
for the howl and the moan
the scream that wouldn't let them near me
the scent of lavender, the music
now ridiculous
in its inability
to reach beyond my skin
into the space
where you were.
I tore at the wires
they strapped onto me
screamed with a widened mouth
stretched demon-shaped
and open

[. . . .]

as god.
Everyone who wanted
to help
retreated
in the face
of the fierceness, the helplessness
the space that opened farther
and farther
into me
with you inside
pounding
                    no
                              way
                                        out.

Noon in Neverland

Noon in neverland; white table, ceiling,
screen in my face. Tubes and limbs unaware
but pressure of you
inside me, moving.
I swear I feel the knife but the face above me
says impossible. I hold my breath,
he says to breathe, here comes
a pressing down, then up—
but nothing prepares me for the moment I transform
from your vessel/sacred space to
opened empty
womb and you
floating
in the air: face screwed up
into the wail
until I kiss you
my future
familiar
here
in the white space
between lives.

Redbud

We carry the placenta home
in a bucket
to plant your tree, redbud
with red blood congealed tissue
that fed you
oxygen.
We put it in the earth, you looking on
from my knee.

You move from one organ
to another
uterus, breast,
molecules move out of me
as I empty
into you
fill you
as you fill the nights
with restlessness, cheek on my breast
leg on my leg
you overflow into the dark
make every crevice, every wrinkle
alive with breath and sound.
You reach for me without waking
your mouth finds my breast
and you drink
beyond what I imagine
I can hold.

We see it out the window
while holding you in our arms
the stretching and the reaching out
the smallest reddest
flowering leaves
the way it drinks the rain
and stores it
for the drought.

5 Nights

1.

Adrenaline plays the accordion
of my ribs
compressing and releasing
my heart
chasing sleep

2.

Sweet baby sleeping on my arm
open lips exhaling
love

3.

Daddy with sling over head and arm
rocking baby to Van Morrison
circling the room

4.

Little bits of mucous
pasted on his nose and chin
like tiny diamonds

5.

On the beach tonight
under moon, he loves to utter
its name
he saw big water
the size of sky

Begin

I.

Begin with the cup
of wine we shared
years ago, on the battlefield
the Kiddush cup
before the breaking glass, mazel tov
the metal cup we drank from
hair trembling in the wind
lips soft, closing
on the rim.

The cup transforms to crystal
your grandmother left
broken
in places
kept in the cupboard, dusty, alone
our fingers too strong and rough
for the stems, the petals of glass.

And now the cup is plastic
small
with two smiling lips biting down
saying no
he wants to drink from what we have
breakable and heavy.
The wonder of water

with ice
without
with straw or without
small fingers reaching in
the cup
upending it
emptying water
over the side
of the chair
the floor,
trickling from his chin.
He is the Zen master
emptying the cup
our cup
making room
always
for more.

II.

Begin with the breath
quick and panted
crying "laa, laa, laa" into
the room that holds
us all
in its cradle
the room we hardly leave for weeks.

[. . .]

Then the breath between his lips
and new protruding teeth
pushed into ga and da and ma
and move, and moon, and more.
He spills words
into the night
in the morning opens his eyes
slowly
to the rising light
unwraps the room, the world
a cup
empty, held out
for more.

Protection

You have my skin, easily bruised
my temper, things you will not
abide.
I want nothing more
than for you to unfold
petal by petal, rising up from the core
like Venus from the sea.
I offer you tools
to sculpt yourself, chisels
with the ends
filed off
so you will not hurt your teeth.
But it is difficult
to pick at stone with metal dull as mud.
This is my paradox
standing guard at the open door
urging you on with one hand on your shirt
hovering
above your choreography
trying to tease out
the you from the me
the definition from destruction
the stumble from the fall.

Expectancy

Sunday morning
he wakes me with kisses
and hugs
at 6 a.m.,
holds me
with his smallest softest arms
the thin blue light
of dawn
outlining the window shades.
"I want to be with you everywhere
you go," he says
skin glowing in the lifting dark.
He smiles as he kisses my head.

He knows our friend is sick
in California
makes her amulets of felt and snow
tells me he's sending her
"woo-hoo medicine"
medicine that will make her better
than anything else
she's tried.
He sings while he works.

She hasn't told her own children
yet
as the days tick slowly empty.
Her hair will fall out.

She searches for a language to explain this
the months of her expectancy
slip backwards
out of reach.
In 9 months she will likely be
in the ground.

She carried each child
daughter, son
when time moved forward toward launching them
each in their own new skin.
And now she is expecting
again.

She gets smaller
with every passing day.
They do not know what to think.
She tells them
nothing.
She struggles to create
a sentence
spends the middle of the night on clauses and predicate,
the morning on prepositions.

It's 3 a.m. there.
There's no blue light
she's awake alone
the products of her last
expectancies

[. . .]

still sleeping in their own rooms,
the new one
growing and developing
not in her uterus
but in her chest
squeezing her with its own small arms
counting the days
with her
and singing as it reaches
toward its own full potential
going with her
everywhere she goes.

In Loco Parentis

In place of me, a school of fish
swimming close, yellow bodies
touchable on every side
they shield you though they know the whale
skims their edges at every turn.
Some change sex, when needed
to keep going.

In place of me, a mother bear
between you and the other
glint of teeth
as she stands sideways, sizing up
you clinging to the bark
waiting in the tree.

In place of me
no stranger
with smooth hands
only the possum
moving in the shadows
carrying you
on her back
the blackbird
to bring you food
the wolf
under the moon.

Chapel

You wear your pajamas
one sock
on the floor with a dinosaur puzzle
still in its box. You lift the lid.
It's time to go.
It's been time to go for 20 minutes.
You don't move.

Your day opens to you slowly
like a door.
It's still ajar, the morning light
weak
and inviting.
You greet it like a druid
still in your sleep clothes
with rituals of play
taking lids off of bins
opening boxes.
"Who will play with me?" you ask.

I was an only child too
but lived in a neighborhood
where children ran like dogs.
At 5 you are alone in your chapel
its architect
you build the sets for every scene
need other players for the parts.
I tell you it's time to go
and you slam doors

then are sorry
to be on the other side.

I want to lead you out into the light
put my hands
under your feet
push you up to the sky
like I don't know
of Icarus
just close my eyes
and feel the shadow pull across my face
as you pass by.

But you're wearing one sock
and I don't have time
and the only thing
that crosses my lips
is the sound
of petty consequence
as I push against the door
of the day
pressing you forward along the ground
into the too early
cold of December
listening to you shout
about every box
left unopened
watching the curls
I did not comb
fall across your face.

To My Son at 4

I watch you
perform your ballerina twirls
glorious curls aflutter cross the room.
You play Mother Ginger, over and over
the Nutcracker's Grande Madame
a dozen children beneath her skirts
transgender mother
of us all.
You say it's her music you love best
but how sorry you are
in versions where she does not appear.

I try to take you to ballet
classes
but you don't need lessons
in how to point your toes
or suburban directresses telling you
t-shirt and black pants
while the girls are draped in taffeta and pink.
Your favorite color is pink.

I write your preschool teacher
to let her know
you've asked to wear bows in your hair
just so she is not surprised.
I get no answer
corner her at parent teacher night a week
after the fact.
She says she's still thinking

about how to respond.
You don't need a response
you wear
what you want
dance in parking lots
and bathrooms.
You break
every box.

At the library in our little
Tea Party town
in the backwoods of New Jersey
your father meets a boy
with Christmas bows in his hair.
His two mothers
are concerned
it's something they
neglected
to do
breathe amazement
at you holding your father's hand
spinning and twirling
makeshift skirt
tied around your waist.
And the two of you, our boys,
run rampant through the library
bows and skirts afloat
on the air
oblivious to the librarians

[. . .]

shaking their heads
fingers to their lips
telling you
to move
more slowly.

Little Goat-Boy

Gray calls to tell me
to expect
a large charge for shoes
on the credit card.
He's visiting his mother
with our son
little Pan-like creature
long mantle of curls
referred to as she
by store clerks and waiters
happily inhabiting
the space in-between
part boy, part girl
part billy goat.

The grandmother offers to buy him shoes.
They pick out sneakers
sky blue
that reminds him
of painted nails
that reminds her of gym mats, class colors.
She puts them on the counter.
Next, she brings him to the boots
pulls down a pair awash in frogs
but he's eying the ones
with the lady bugs.
Perhaps she's not aware
that lady bugs are not
all ladies

[. . .]

tells him no
holds them high above her head
puts them on a shelf he cannot reach.
He cries and his father
takes the lady bug boots
to the counter to pay
his mother yelling from behind
if he buys them she's not getting
the sneakers.

I'll look for them both
on the statement, I say
imagining
my little goat-boy
splashing through the streets
of Boston
covered in lady bugs
jumping in puddles
alive and kicking
in our hybrid world.

Spirits

The psychic says my child's spirit
is female
apologizes for saying she
tells me he talks to fairies, gnomes
is sensitive to spirits.
I know, I nod and reassure her,
I know.

Later I tell him
she says he'll be a medium
he exclaims happily that he's a "middle"
asks me if she knows about
the giant toad spirit
in the woods.

We tell each other
almost everything
but there are things
he doesn't say
out loud.
He bucks against the walls
of my illness
rages
when I can't get out of bed.
When pressed he says he's anxious
about our friend who died last year.
Thinking of her kids
I state the obvious
color in

[. . .]

the chalk outline
of my body supine on the bed
ask him if he's afraid
frustrated
by my always being sick.
He insists it's unrelated
rages day and night
until I rise again
sit at the table
for a meal.
He is suddenly
sanguine.

The giant toad spirit
calls to him
genderless and free
invisible
to everyone else's eyes.

The psychic told me more
a child
who died in an accident
is with
my little one
plays games with him, protects him.
I tell him only
there's a spirit
watching over him.

He says he knows, reminds me
about the toad.

The psychic asked me
who the child was
where was
the accident.
I said I didn't know.

When the school bus crashed
on the highway near our house
knocked clear off its axels
I threw away the paper as soon as it arrived.
Coming in from school, he told me
someone said
that everyone had died.
I assured him
it wasn't true.
When he asked,
"Then everyone's ok?"
I smiled
asked him
if he finished his homework
pulled him close to my body
kissed his head.

Acknowledgments

"House," "I'll Tell You How It Was," "Noon in Neverland," "Expectancy," "Chapel," and "Little Goat-Boy" first appeared in *Lips*.

Praise for Protection

Michelle Lerner's debut chapbook *Protection* is a breathtaking poetic journey of pregnancy and motherhood. I love Lerner's luminous imagery that fuses at times with an unexpected searing irony. There is an originality of subject matter and candor dealing with exploring gender identity of children that reinforces this author's openness and intelligence. Her poem "House" may be the fiercest and most tender poem about pregnancy I've ever read. Michelle Lerner is a new shimmering star on our poetry planet.

—Laura Boss, author of *The Best Lover,*
editor of *Lips*

Michelle Lerner's Chapbook of poems, *Protection*, explores the relationship between parents and their unborn child and traces it to the child's development as a separate human being with the freedom to choose an identity. These are beautiful lyric narratives that touch the heart.

—Maria Mazziotti Gillan,
American book award winner and poet,
author of *Blooms in Winter,*
editor of *Paterson Literary Review*

The title poem in Michelle Lerner's lovely and nuanced chapbook, *Protection*, speaks of teasing out "the definition from destruction/ the stumble from the fall." This theme of the necessary danger of experience is central in these bold poems on parenting and its discoveries. Searching from within the personal and the wider world the poems create a vivid and moving portrait of a life in our moment, written with vulnerability, insight, and a keen eye for fresh, revealing detail."

—Jennifer Michael Hecht, Ph.D.,
author of *Who Said* (Copper Canyon)

About the Author

Michelle Lerner is a recovering public interest lawyer and cat herder. She's currently raising a magpie-like child while emerging from the depths of late-stage chronic Lyme Disease, writing songs on a shiny new guitar, and unsuccessfully trying to establish a disciplined schedule to work on her poetry and fiction.

She received an MFA in poetry from The New School and her poetry manuscripts have been selected as finalist for The Poetry Box® Chapbook Prize and semifinalist for the 2018 Pamet River Prize and the 2020 Willow Run Poetry Book Award. Her individual poems have appeared in many journals and other fora, including *VQR's* Instagram Series, *Harvard Women's Law Journal*, *Paterson Literary Review*, *Lips*, *Adanna*, *Knock*, and *Sixfold*, as well as several anthologies.

The manuscript for her debut novel, *Ring*, has been selected as a finalist for Book Pipeline's Unpublished Contest and the Bridge Eight Fiction Prize, longlisted for the Dzanc Prize for Fiction, and chosen as a Notable Selection for the Chapter One Prize, while it awaits a publisher.

Michelle recently became a writing mentor for We Are Not Numbers, a nonprofit that publishes the autobiographical stories of Palestinians living under occupation and in refugee camps. <wearenotnumbers.org>

About The Poetry Box®

The Poetry Box® is a boutique publishing company in Portland, Oregon, which provides a platform for both established and emerging poets to share their words with the world through beautiful printed books and chapbooks.

Feel free to visit the online bookstore (thePoetryBox.com), where you'll find more titles including:

Matrimony by Laurel Feigenbaum

Nothing More to Lose by Carolyn Martin

Staring Down the Tracks by Julia Paul

Notes from a Caregiver by Meg Lindsay

Like the O in Hope by Jeanne Julian

A Shape of Sky by Cathy Cain

The Very Rich Hours by Gregory Loselle

Catching Narcissus by Rheanna Haaland

Just the Girls by Pamela R. Anderson-Bartholet

Between States of Matter by Sherry Rind

The Kingdom of Birds by Joan Colby

Building a Woman by Deborah Meltvedt

My Mother Never Died Before by Marcia B. Loughran

Off Coldwater Canyon by C.W. Emerson

Mouth Quill by Kaja Weeks

and more . . .

www.ingramcontent.com/pod-product-compliance
Ingram Content Group UK Ltd.
Pitfield, Milton Keynes, MK11 3LW, UK
UKHW040028200726
13854UKWH00001B/413

9 781948 461887